Songs for Children

Teacher Gwynneth D. Walker

Illustrated By: Jody H. Darrow

Copyright 2001 by Althea N. Martin
Copyright © 2020 by Gwynneth D. Walker

Paperback: 978-1-63767-095-8
Hardcover: 978-1-63767-144-3
eBook: 978-1-63767-094-1
Library of Congress Control Number: 2021903581

All rights reserved. No part of this publication may be reproduced, distributed, or transmitted in any form or by any electronic or mechanical means, without the prior written permission of the publisher, except in the case of brief quotations embodied in critical reviews and certain other noncommercial uses permitted by copyright law.

The views expressed in this work are solely those of the author and do not necessarily reflect the views of the publisher, and the publisher hereby disclaims any responsibility for them.

Ordering Information:

BookTrail Agency
8838 Sleepy Hollow Rd.
Kansas City, MO 64114

Printed in the United States of America

Table of Contents

I'm a Little Bluebird 5

Buttercups 6

Little Caterpillar 7

The Squirrel 9

Pretty Lady Daffodil 11

October 13

The Storm 14

Raindrops 15

May Day 17

School Boy 18

Grandmother (Also Grandfather) 19

Sing a Song of Friendship 20

Hello Spring 21

Turkey Gobbler 22

Reindeer 23

Valentine 24

Patty's Day Dance 25

Easter Bunny 26

George Washington 27

Circle Time 29

I'm a Little Bluebird

Words and Melody by:
Gwynneth Walker

I'm a lit-tle blue-bird. Lis-ten to my song!
My time I spend sing-ing; I'm hap-py all day long.

Buttercups

**Words and Melody by:
Gwynneth Walker**

I know that spring is here, be-cause I hear the rob-ins sing,

And all the lit-tle but-ter cups, are danc-ing in a ring.

Little Caterpillar

Words and Melody by:
Gwynneth Walker

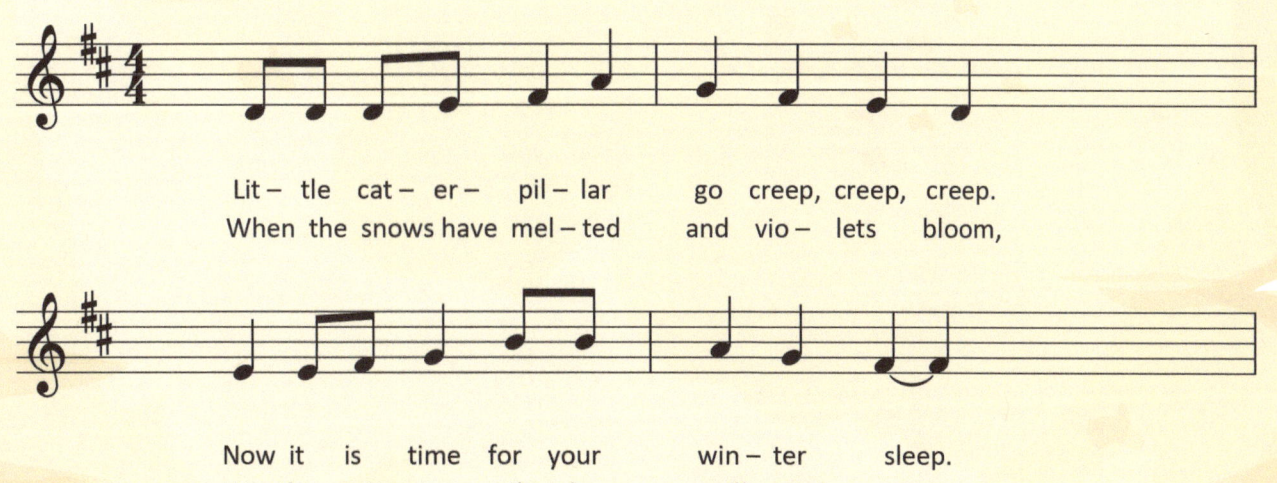

Lit — tle cat — er — pil — lar   go creep, creep, creep.
When the snows have mel — ted   and vio — lets bloom,

Now it is time for your   win — ter sleep.
Lit — tle cat — er — pil — lar   you'll need more room.

The Squirrel

Words and Melody by:
Gwynneth Walker

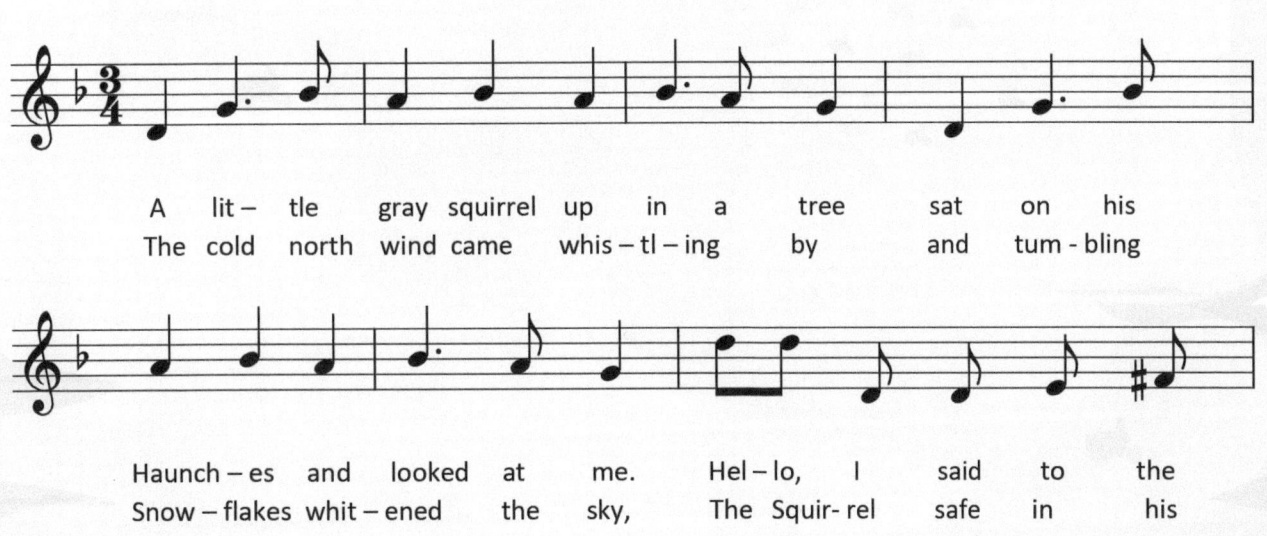

A lit – tle gray squirrel up in a tree sat on his
The cold north wind came whis – tl – ing by and tum - bling

Haunch – es and looked at me. Hel – lo, I said to the
Snow – flakes whit – ened the sky, The Squir- rel safe in his

Pretty Lady Daffodil

Words and Melody by:
Gwynneth Walker

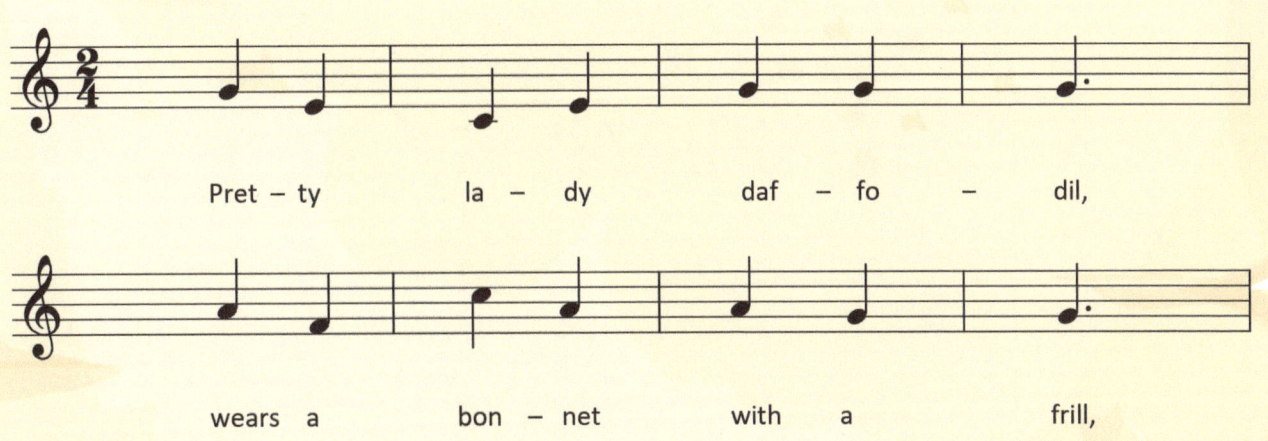

Pret — ty   la — dy   daf — fo — dil,

wears a   bon — net   with a   frill,

October

Words and Melody by:
Gwynneth Walker

The Storm

Words and Melody by:
Gwynneth Walker

Hear the thun – der crash! See the light – ning flash!
Ea – ger – ly the flowers drink the fall – ing rain.

Watch the pret – ty rain – drops fall, soon the storm will pass.
There's a rain – bow in the sky. It is clear a – gain.

Raindrops

Words and Melody by:
Gwynneth Walker

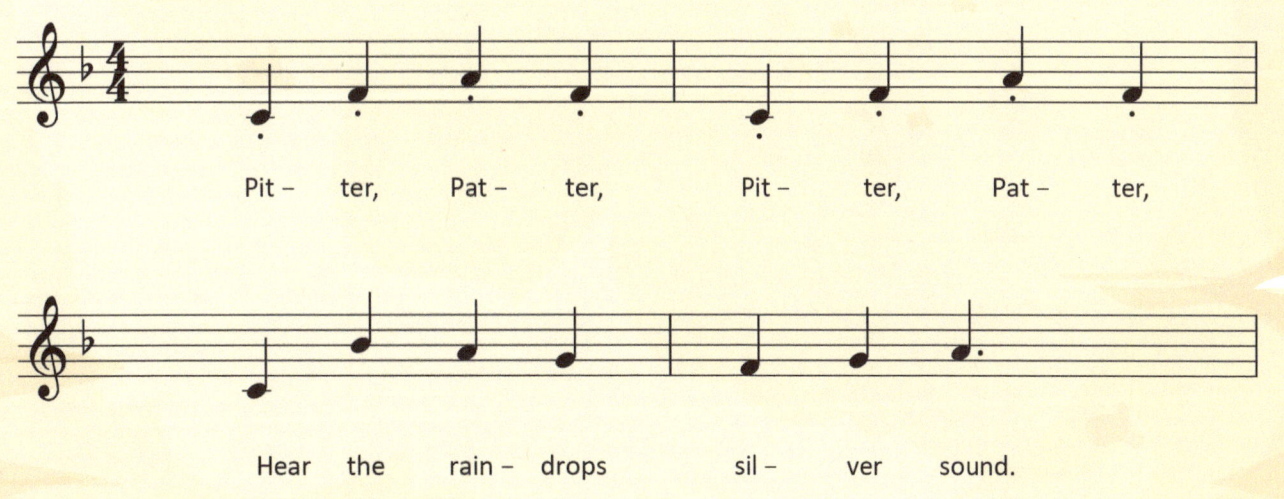

Pit – ter, Pat – ter, Pit – ter, Pat – ter,

Hear the rain – drops sil – ver sound.

May Day

**Words and Melody by:
Gwynneth Walker**

School Boy

Words and Melody by:
Gwynneth Walker

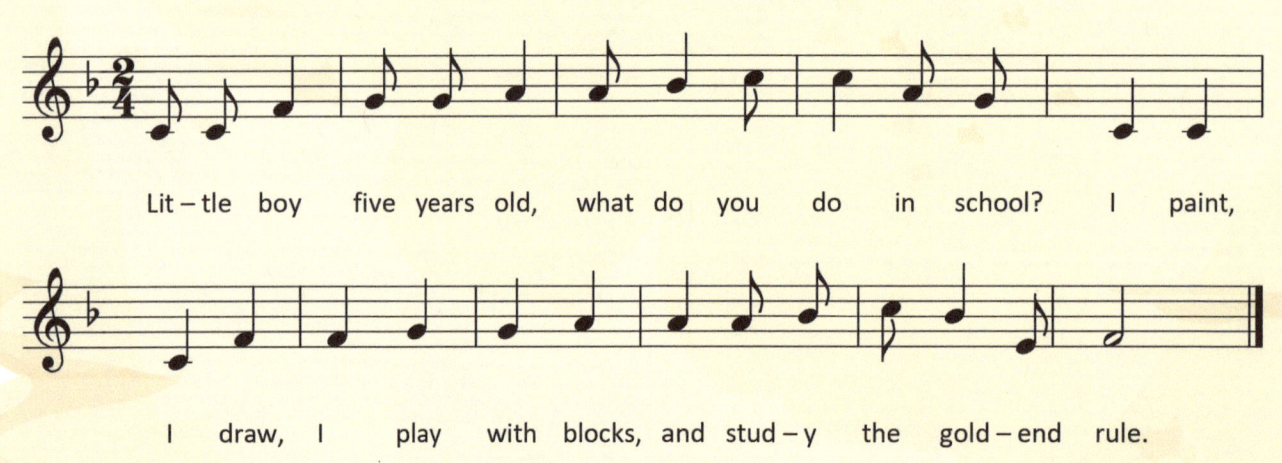

Lit—tle boy five years old, what do you do in school? I paint,
I draw, I play with blocks, and stud—y the gold—end rule.

Grandmother (Also Grandfather)

Words and Melody by:
Gwynneth Walker

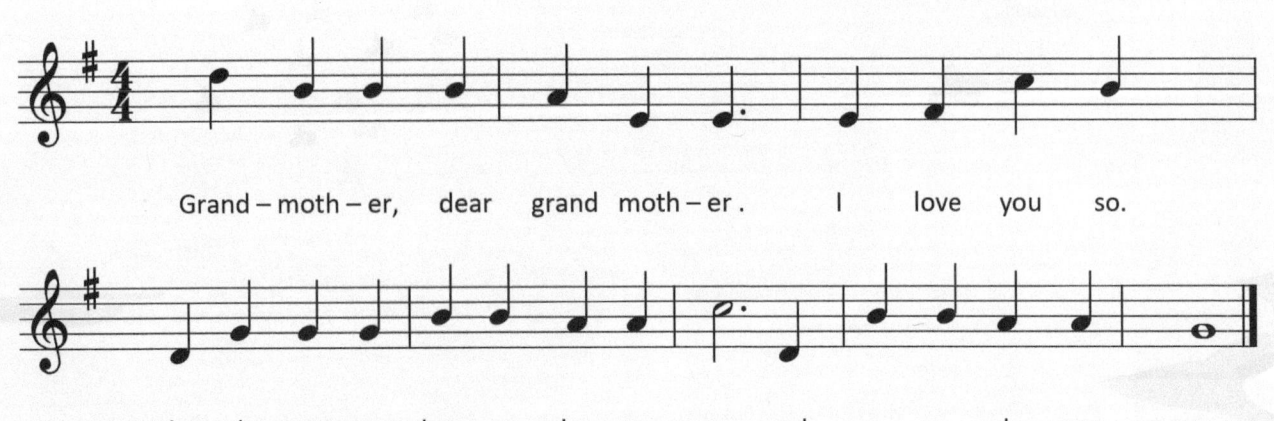

Grand—moth—er, dear grand moth—er. I love you so.

I'm al—ways so hap—py when you come, and sor—ry when you go.

Sing a Song of Friendship

Words by Gwynneth Walker
Melody - Sing a Song of Sixpence

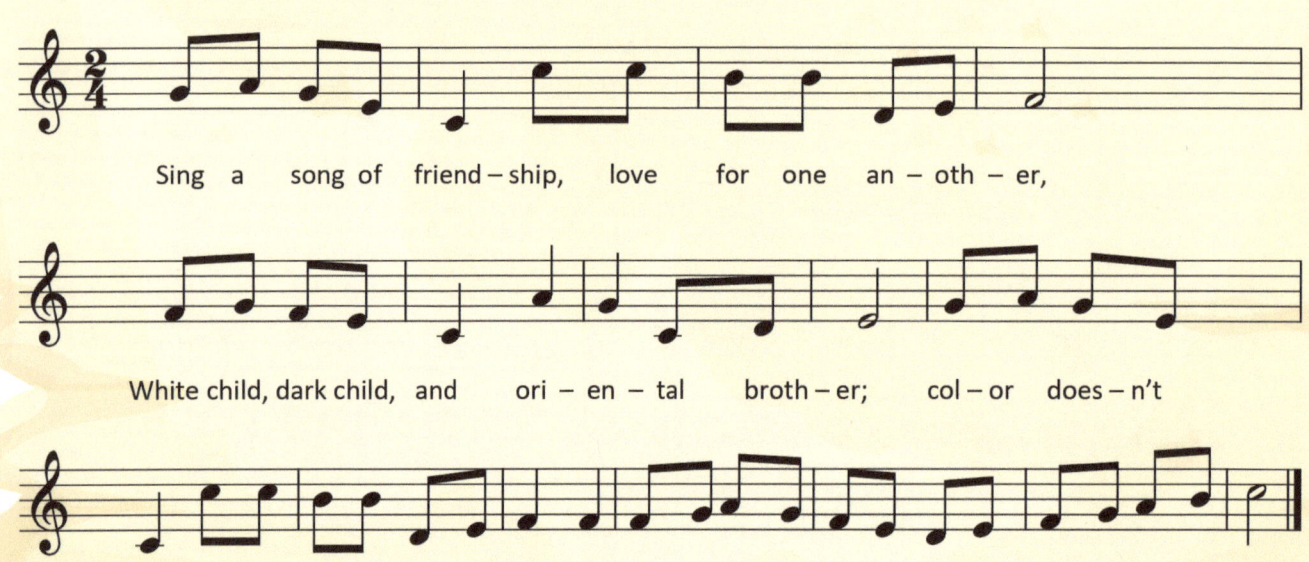

Sing a song of friend-ship, love for one an-oth-er,

White child, dark child, and ori-en-tal broth-er; col-or does-n't

Mat-ter, It's just an-oth-er name, our Fath-er made us, one and all, and loves us just the same

Hello Spring

Words and Melody by:
Gwynneth Walker

The air is warm and the sky is blue. The leaves are light green be- cause they're new.

Your feet go skip –ping the bird all sing. The whole world is hap – py be-cause it is spring.

Turkey Gobbler

Words and Melody by:
Gwynneth Walker

Gob – ble, Gob – ble who is that? Tur – key gob – bler big and fat.

Gob – ble, Gob – ble what does he say? Meet me on Thanks – giv – ing day.

Reindeer

**Words and Melody by:
Gwynneth Walker**

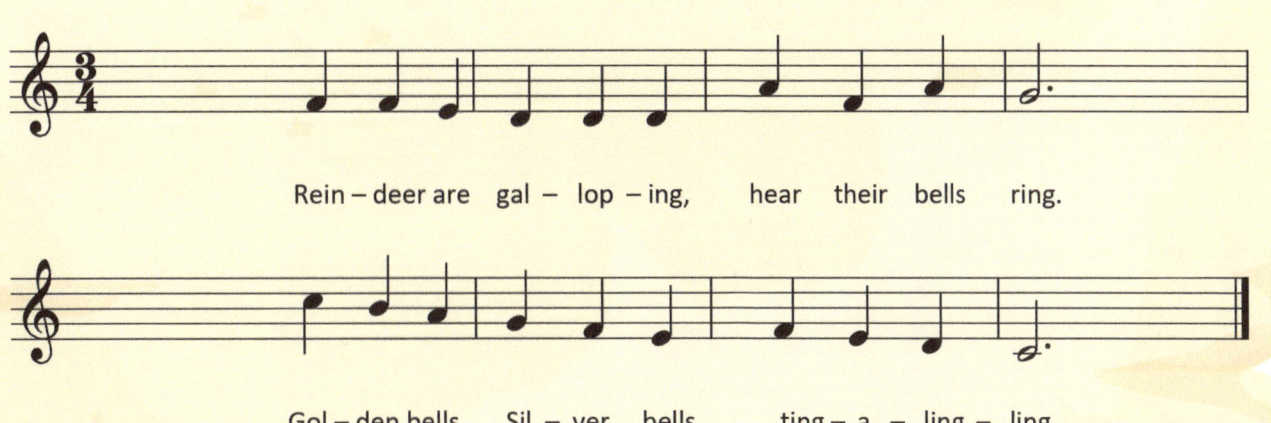

Rein – deer are gal – lop – ing,   hear   their   bells   ring.

Gol – den bells , Sil – ver   bells   ting – a – ling – ling.

Valentine

**Words and Melody by:
Gwynneth Walker**

Val – en – tine, Val – en – tine If you'll be mine.

Val – en – tine, Val – en – tine I will be thine.

Patty's Day Dance

Words and Melody by:
Gwynneth Walker

On Pat – ty's Day we dance a jig, all dressed in I – rish green.

Toe, heel, Kick - Toe, heel, Kick - Pat and his fair col - leen.

Easter Bunny

Words and Melody by:
Gwynneth Walker

The East–ter Bun–ny goes hip–pi–ty hop, and hip–pi–ty hop he goes,

Bus–i–ly hid–ing the East–er eggs. Now what has he hid–den for me?

George Washington

Words and Melody by:
Gwynneth Walker

Geor – gie had a hat – chet, a new lit – tle hat – chet.

Geor – gie had a hat – chet, he like it ver – y much.

Circle Time

**Words and Melody by:
Gwynneth Walker**

Once up – on a time a dear lit – tle clown

Lived in a school in Had – don field town.

Biography

Gwynneth Dorothy Rosalind Walker was born on January 15, 1906 in Birtle, a small town, in the Province of Manitoba, Canada. She was the youngest of the seven children in this family. They were all born in England with the exception of Gwynneth.

The family moved to Brooklyn, New York, when she was one month old. Gwynneth attended a Brooklyn elementary school until the age of ten. The family then moved to Haddonfield, New Jersey, where they resided permanently.

Upon graduating from Haddonfield High School she attended the University of North Carolina for a short time. Later, Gwynneth enrolled in classes at the Moore Institute of Art in Philadelphia, Pennsylvania and took courses in Early Childhood Education at Glassboro College and at Rutgers University in New Jersey.

Gwynneth loved her work with the little children at the Haddonfield Friends School where she taught until her death. She devoted her life to the Pre-kindergarten classroom. The "Curriculum" she presented instilled a love of nature and an appreciation of language through her original poetry. She was, also, an artist who further expressed her love of nature through paintings of out-door scenery.

Although she passed away in 1964 at the age of fifty-eight years, Gwynneth has left a legacy to all boys and girls through her poetry. The verses are ageless in their appeal and, hopefully, will be enjoyed by future generations of your children.

a.n.m

Jody H. Darrow's artistic gift from God was first recognized when she was a child by her father; a master printer and owner of the Hibbert Printing Co. of Trenton, NJ. The business was lost during the "Great Depression." Several years later her father passed away.

Lack of finances prevented any further education for Jody but her love of art and talent kept her actively interested in drawing. Through the years she illustrated catalogs, posters, murals, books and stories at an amateur level. Humbly, she believed that her lack of formal education limited her horizons.

Jody's public relations positions at the Washington Crossing Foundation gave her the opportunity to be considered semi-professional. When Althea N. Martin asked her to do the illustrations for the books by Gwynneth D. Walker, Jody felt she attained a professional level.

The illustrations, undoubtedly, have enhanced the wonderful verses of the books and will entertain children and adults for many years.

Althea N. Martin, a dedicated school psychologist, was very impressed with Teacher Gwynneth D. Walker when her daughter attended Haddonfield Friends School pre-kindergarten class. Every year a "Spring Frolic" was held in May where each class presented a sketch or activity in tribute to Spring. One year Teacher Gwynneth had each child in her class dress as a flower and little Althea was a white rose.

Upon the untimely death of Gwynneth D. Walker, Althea, Sr. recognized the value of the poetry and songs that Gwynneth had created. She felt that they should not be lost and was granted permission by the Walker family to compile and copyright her material.

The seven books, compiled from Teacher Gwynneth's work, have been enhanced with the illustrations by Jody H. Darrow. Althea, Sr. searched for many years before this dream was finally realized.

May the words, music and thoughts created by Teacher Gwynneth live on for future children and adults to enjoy. All who love nature's beauty, poetry, and songs will be blessed to have the legacy of Gwynneth D. Walker touch their lives.

Milton Keynes UK
Ingram Content Group UK Ltd.
UKHW021226160324
439623UK00003B/11